WELCOME TO THE U.S.A.
PENNSYLVANIA

Written by Ann Heinrichs   Illustrated by Matt Kania
Content Adviser: Kathy Hale, Library Development Adviser,
State Library of Pennsylvania, Harrisburg, Pennsylvania

The Child's World

Published in the United States of America by The Child's World®
PO Box 326 • Chanhassen, MN 55317-0326
800-599-READ • www.childsworld.com

Photo Credits
Cover: Getty Images/The Image Bank/Francesco Ruggeri; frontispiece: Photodisc.

Interior: Amish Farm and House: 13; AP/Wide World Photos/H. Rumph, Jr.: 17; Carnegie Science Center: 26; Corbis: 9 (Reuters), 30 (Bob Krist); Erie Maritime Museum: 18; Getty Images: 14 (William Thomas Cain), 29 (The Image Bank/Jurgen Vogt), 34 (Elsa); The Hershey Company: 33; Mike Husarik/Tour-Ed Mine: 22; Lenni Lenape Historical Society: 10; Library of Congress: 16, 27; Photodisc: 6, 21; The Railroader's Memorial Museum: 25.

Acknowledgments
The Child's World®: Mary Berendes, Publishing Director

Editorial Directions, Inc.: E. Russell Primm, Editorial Director; Katie Marsico, Associate Editor; Judith Shiffer, Assistant Editor; Matt Messbarger, Editorial Assistant; Susan Hindman, Copy Editor; Melissa McDaniel, Proofreader; Kevin Cunningham, Peter Garnham, Matt Messbarger, Olivia Nellums, Chris Simms, Molly Symmonds, Katherine Trickle, Carl Stephen Wender, Fact Checkers; Tim Griffin/IndexServ, Indexer; Cian Loughlin O'Day, Photo Researcher and Editor

The Design Lab: Kathleen Petelinsek, Design; Julia Goozen, Art Production

Library of Congress Cataloging-in-Publication Data
Heinrichs, Ann.
  Pennsylvania / by Ann Heinrichs ; cartography and illustrations by Matt Kania.
    p. cm. — (Welcome to the U.S.A.)
  Includes index.
  ISBN 1-59296-480-X (library bound : alk. paper)
  1. Pennsylvania—Juvenile literature. I. Kania, Matt, ill. II. Title.
  F149.3.H463 2006
  974.8—dc22   2005008820

Ann Heinrichs is the author of more than 100 books for children and young adults. She has also enjoyed successful careers as a children's book editor and an advertising copywriter. Ann grew up in Fort Smith, Arkansas, and lives in Chicago, Illinois.

About the Author
Ann Heinrichs

Matt Kania loves maps and, as a kid, dreamed of making them. In school he studied geography and cartography, and today he makes maps for a living. Matt's favorite thing about drawing maps is learning about the places they represent. Many of the maps he has created can be found in books, magazines, videos, Web sites, and public places.

About the
Map Illustrator
Matt Kania

On the cover: You can see the historic Liberty Bell in Philadelphia.
On page one: Three rivers come together in the city of Pittsburgh.

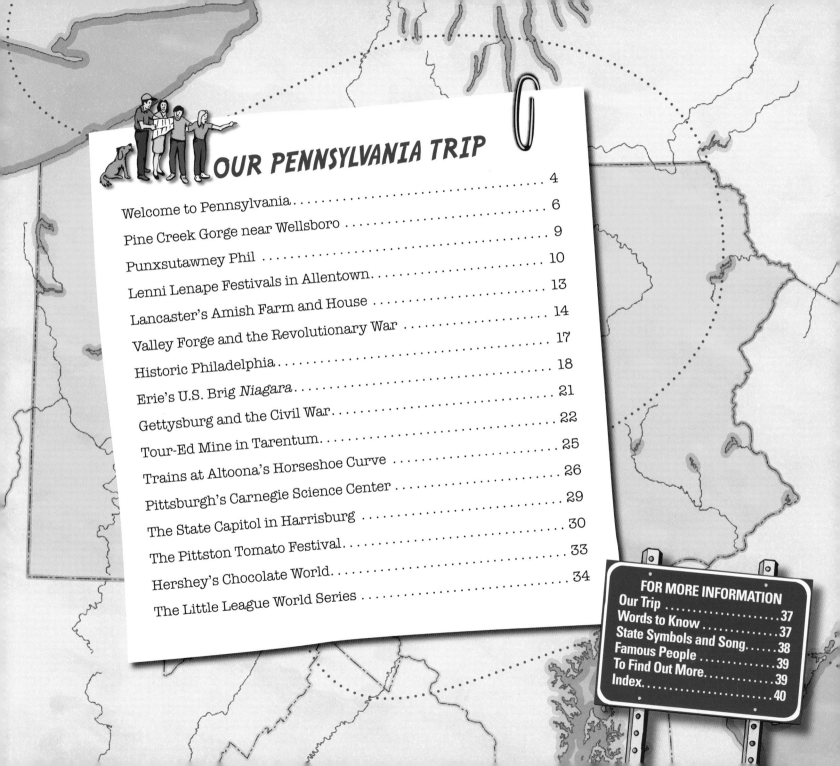

OUR PENNSYLVANIA TRIP

Pennsylvania's Nickname:
The Keystone State

Let's take a trip through Pennsylvania. You'll have some great adventures there!

You'll board a sailing ship and tour a mine. You'll see battlefields and soldiers' huts. You'll meet Benjamin Franklin and Andrew Carnegie. You'll stand right next to the Liberty Bell. You'll explore mountains, forests, and **canyons.** You'll tour a chocolate factory. And you'll meet a friendly groundhog named Phil!

Are you ready? Then settle in and buckle up. Pennsylvania, here we come!

WELCOME TO PENNSYLVANIA

As you travel through Pennsylvania, watch for all the interesting facts along the way.

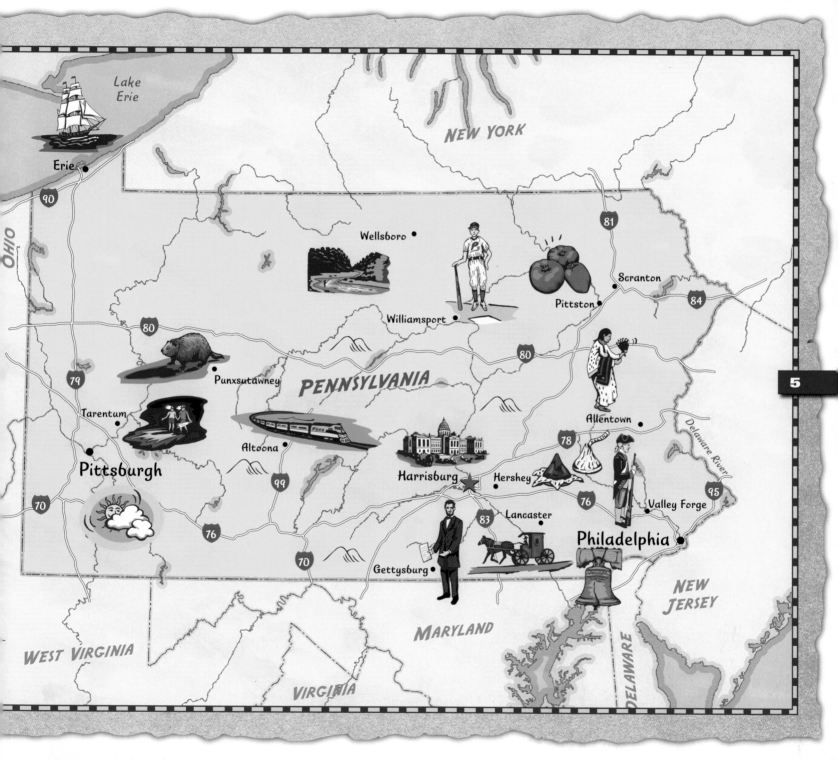

Lake Erie

NEW YORK

Erie

OHIO

90

81

Wellsboro

Scranton

Pittston

84

Williamsport

80

Punxsutawney

PENNSYLVANIA

79

Tarentum

Altoona

Allentown

Delaware River

78

Pittsburgh

99

Harrisburg

Hershey

76

Valley Forge

95

70

76

83

Lancaster

Philadelphia

Gettysburg

MARYLAND

NEW JERSEY

70

WEST VIRGINIA

DELAWARE

VIRGINIA

The fish in Pine Creek get really big! Try to catch some for yourself at this scenic spot

Pine Creek Gorge near Wellsboro

Stand atop a rocky ridge. Then look down the mountainside. Rushing waters are roaring hundreds of feet below.

You're gazing down Pine Creek Gorge. It's on the Allegheny **Plateau.** This region covers northern and western Pennsylvania. It's part of the Appalachian Mountain range. The Allegheny Mountains rise at its eastern edge.

The Pocono Mountains are in northeastern Pennsylvania. They have many beautiful waterfalls. The land in the southeast is lower.

Three rivers come together in Pittsburgh. They're the Ohio, Allegheny, and Monongahela rivers. The Delaware River forms Pennsylvania's eastern border.

The Delaware Water Gap is a recreation area. It runs along part of the Delaware River.

LAKE ERIE

NEW YORK

7

Highest Temperature: Phoenixville July 10, 1936 111°F (44°C)

Lowest Temperature: Smethport January 5, 1904 -42°F (-41°C)

• Wellsboro

Smethport

Pine Creek Gorge

Allegheny Plateau

Pocono Mountains

Delaware Water Gap

OHIO

Let's hike the Turkey Path Trail! It goes down to the bottom of the gorge. We'll pass a waterfall on the way!

Allegheny River

Ohio River

Allegheny Mountains

Appalachian Mountains

Delaware River

NEW JERSEY

• Pittsburgh

Monongahela River

Mount Davis

Phoenixville •

HIGHEST AND LOWEST POINTS
Highest: Mount Davis at 3,213 feet (979 m)
Lowest: Sea level along the Delaware River

Pine Creek Gorge is called the Grand Canyon of Pennsylvania. The real Grand Canyon is in Arizona.

MARYLAND

WEST VIRGINIA

Pennsylvania's northwest corner borders Lake Erie. That's one of the country's Great Lakes.

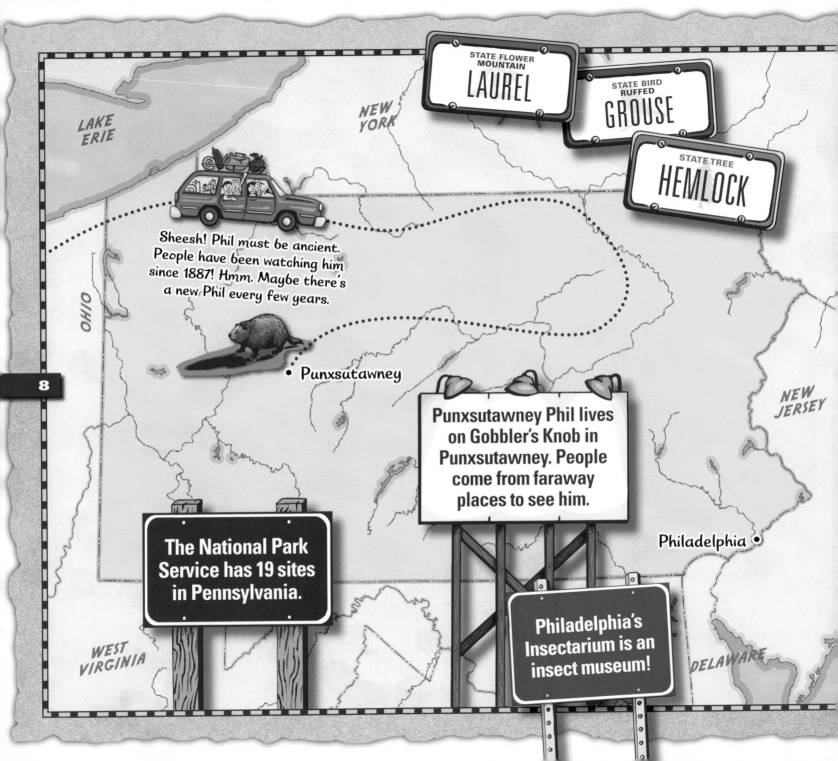

Punxsutawney Phil

Furry little Phil pokes his head out. He looks around and squints. Then he goes back into his hole. Too bad. Six more weeks of winter!

This famous groundhog is Punxsutawney Phil. People watch him on Groundhog Day, which is February 2. Will he see his shadow? If he doesn't, spring is coming. What if he sees it? Then winter's staying for six more weeks!

Many other animals live in Pennsylvania. There are deer, rabbits, wild turkeys, and raccoons. Even black bears roam the woods. But only Phil predicts the weather!

Don't put away your winter coat yet. Punxsutawney Phil spotted his shadow on this sunny day.

Groundhogs hibernate during the winter. That means they go into a kind of deep sleep.

Lenni Lenape Festivals in Allentown

These Lenni Lenape Indians wear traditional dress. They're performing at the Corn Festival.

10

The dancers wear feathers and colorful beads. Some of the feathers look like big wings! You're watching performers at the Lenni Lenape Corn Festival. The Lenni Lenape are a Native American group. They hold festivals at the Lenni Lenape Historical Society.

The Lenni Lenape are also called the Delaware. They've lived in Pennsylvania for hundreds of years. Englishman William Penn arrived in 1682. He bought land from the Indians. He then founded the Pennsylvania **Colony.** It was one of thirteen British colonies.

Penn belonged to the Quaker religious group. He welcomed people of all faiths in Pennsylvania.

William Penn gave Pennsylvania its name. He used the name *Penn*, after his father, and *sylvania*, from *sylvan*. Sylvan means "woods" in Latin.

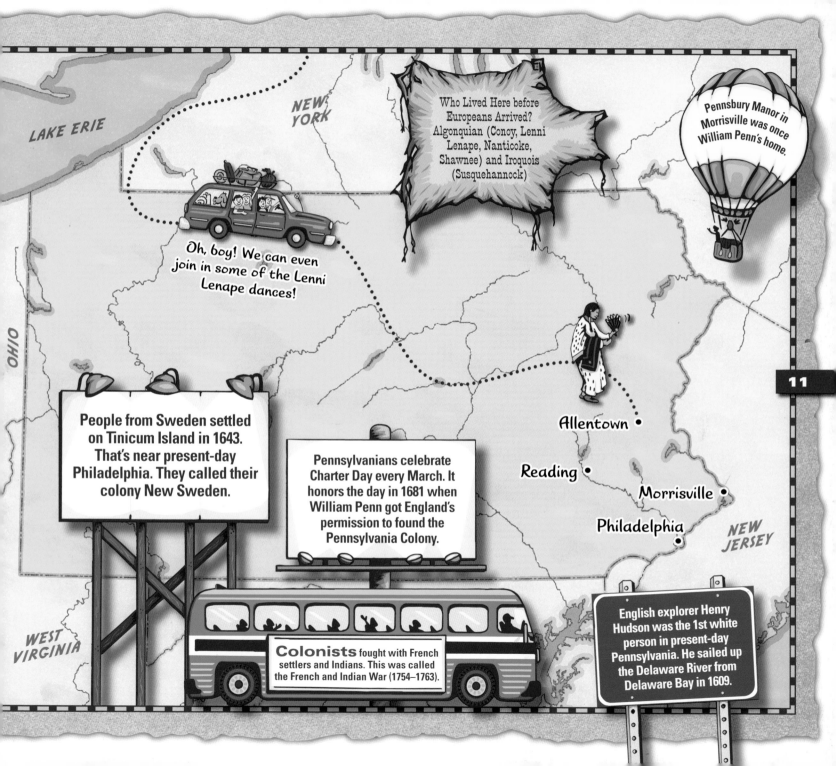

LAKE ERIE

NEW YORK

Who Lived Here before Europeans Arrived? Algonquian (Conoy, Lenni Lenape, Nanticoke, Shawnee) and Iroquois (Susquehannock)

Pennsbury Manor in Morrisville was once William Penn's home.

Oh, boy! We can even join in some of the Lenni Lenape dances!

OHIO

People from Sweden settled on Tinicum Island in 1643. That's near present-day Philadelphia. They called their colony New Sweden.

Pennsylvanians celebrate Charter Day every March. It honors the day in 1681 when William Penn got England's permission to found the Pennsylvania Colony.

Allentown

Reading

Morrisville

Philadelphia

NEW JERSEY

WEST VIRGINIA

Colonists fought with French settlers and Indians. This was called the French and Indian War (1754–1763).

English explorer Henry Hudson was the 1st white person in present-day Pennsylvania. He sailed up the Delaware River from Delaware Bay in 1609.

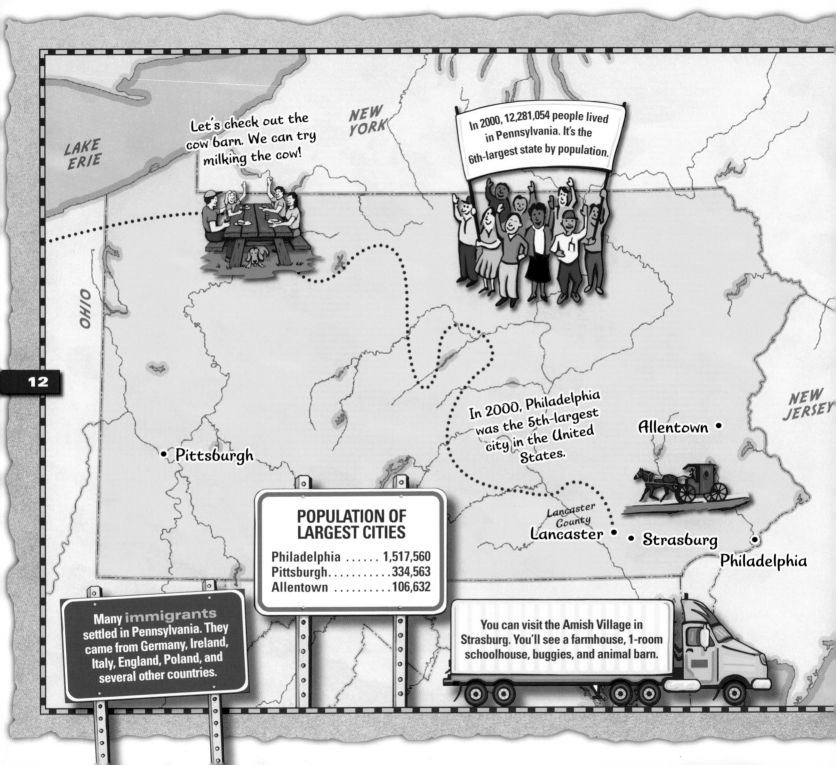

Let's check out the cow barn. We can try milking the cow!

In 2000, 12,281,054 people lived in Pennsylvania. It's the 6th-largest state by population.

LAKE ERIE

NEW YORK

OHIO

NEW JERSEY

In 2000, Philadelphia was the 5th-largest city in the United States.

• Pittsburgh

Allentown •

Lancaster County
Lancaster • • Strasburg

Philadelphia •

POPULATION OF LARGEST CITIES

Philadelphia 1,517,560
Pittsburgh.......... 334,563
Allentown 106,632

Many **immigrants** settled in Pennsylvania. They came from Germany, Ireland, Italy, England, Poland, and several other countries.

You can visit the Amish Village in Strasburg. You'll see a farmhouse, 1-room schoolhouse, buggies, and animal barn.

Lancaster's Amish Farm and House

Stroll around the farm. You'll see the windmill and barns. Cows and horses are grazing. The blacksmith is busy making horseshoes. Then visit the farmhouse. Wooden benches are set up for church services. Simple, dark clothes hang in the bedroom.

You're visiting the Amish Farm and House. The Amish are a Christian religious group. They're sometimes called the Pennsylvania Dutch. William Penn welcomed them to Pennsylvania.

The Amish dress and live in a simple way. They don't use electricity or modern machines. They make most of the things they need. People help their neighbors with heavy chores. Would you like to live this way?

Check out the blacksmith exhibit. Life sure was different without modern machines!

More than 20,000 Amish people live in the Lancaster County area. Their roots are in Germany.

George Washington camped here with soldiers like these. He went on to become our country's 1st president.

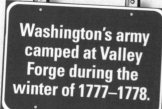

Washington's army camped at Valley Forge during the winter of 1777–1778.

Valley Forge and the Revolutionary War

The colonists grew to hate British taxes. Colonial leaders formed the Continental Congress. They met in Philadelphia in 1774. Some colonists wanted to stay friendly with Britain. Others wanted to fight Britain for freedom. Soon the Revolutionary War (1775–1783) broke out.

General George Washington led the colonial army. Washington's army camped at Valley Forge one winter. It was bitterly cold, and supplies were low. Many soldiers died there.

You can visit Valley Forge today. You'll see the soldiers' log huts. Imagine how bravely they fought for freedom!

The colonial army beat the British at last. The colonies became the United States of America.

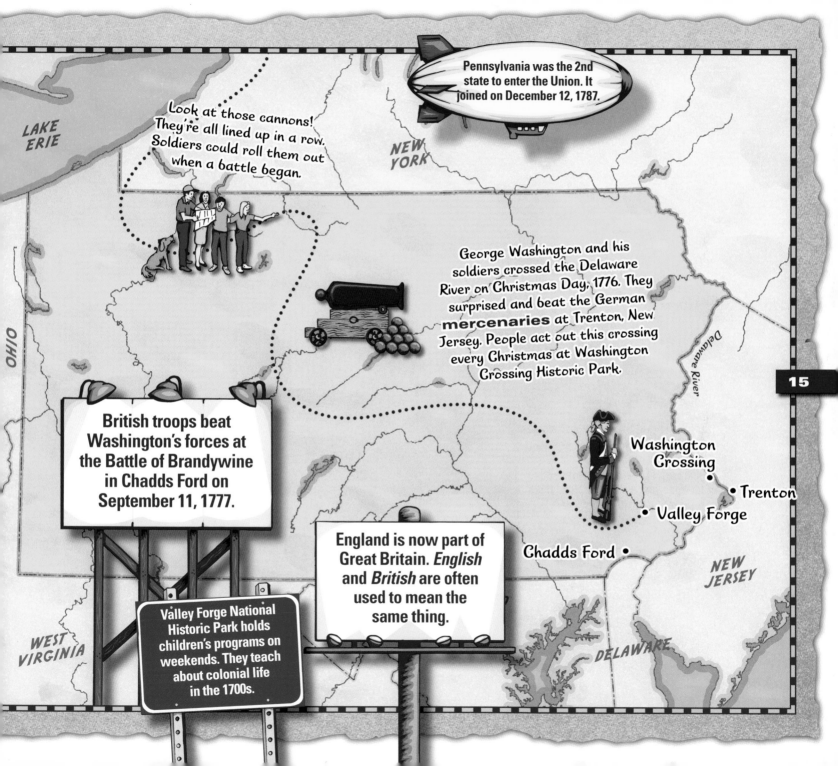

Pennsylvania was the 2nd state to enter the Union. It joined on December 12, 1787.

Look at those cannons! They're all lined up in a row. Soldiers could roll them out when a battle began.

LAKE ERIE

NEW YORK

George Washington and his soldiers crossed the Delaware River on Christmas Day, 1776. They surprised and beat the German **mercenaries** at Trenton, New Jersey. People act out this crossing every Christmas at Washington Crossing Historic Park.

OHIO

Delaware River

British troops beat Washington's forces at the Battle of Brandywine in Chadds Ford on September 11, 1777.

Washington Crossing

• Trenton

• Valley Forge

England is now part of Great Britain. *English* and *British* are often used to mean the same thing.

Chadds Ford •

NEW JERSEY

Valley Forge National Historic Park holds children's programs on weekends. They teach about colonial life in the 1700s.

WEST VIRGINIA

DELAWARE

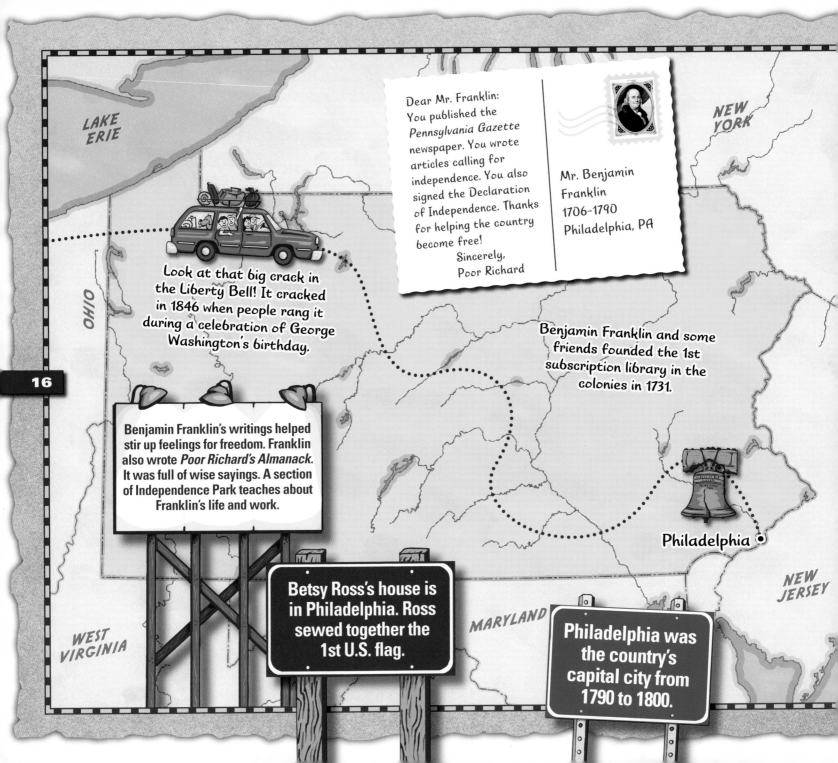

LAKE ERIE

NEW YORK

OHIO

Dear Mr. Franklin:
You published the *Pennsylvania Gazette* newspaper. You wrote articles calling for independence. You also signed the Declaration of Independence. Thanks for helping the country become free!
Sincerely,
Poor Richard

Mr. Benjamin Franklin
1706-1790
Philadelphia, PA

Look at that big crack in the Liberty Bell! It cracked in 1846 when people rang it during a celebration of George Washington's birthday.

Benjamin Franklin and some friends founded the 1st subscription library in the colonies in 1731.

Benjamin Franklin's writings helped stir up feelings for freedom. Franklin also wrote *Poor Richard's Almanack*. It was full of wise sayings. A section of Independence Park teaches about Franklin's life and work.

Philadelphia

WEST VIRGINIA

MARYLAND

NEW JERSEY

Betsy Ross's house is in Philadelphia. Ross sewed together the 1st U.S. flag.

Philadelphia was the country's capital city from 1790 to 1800.

Historic Philadelphia

Stand beside the Liberty Bell. It's bigger than you! And it weighs more than dozens of kids.

This big bell is in Independence National Historical Park. That's Philadelphia's old section. You'll see many historic buildings there. One is Independence Hall. The Declaration of Independence was signed there. The U.S. Constitution was written there, too. It states the country's basic ideas and laws.

The First Continental Congress met in nearby Carpenters' Hall. Just walk along the streets. You'll learn about history without even trying!

Want to see an important piece of history? Visit the Liberty Bell at Independence National Historical Park.

Thomas Jefferson wrote most of the Declaration of Independence. You can visit Philadelphia's Declaration House, where he wrote it.

There goes the *Niagara*! Wave to the crew as it sets sail!

Erie's U.S. Brig *Niagara*

Climb aboard the *Niagara*. It's a sailing ship called a brig. Then imagine you're fighting a sea battle. This ship won a famous battle in 1813.

Commodore Oliver Hazard Perry commanded the *Niagara*. He was fighting in the War of 1812 (1812–1815). Perry beat several British ships on Lake Erie. Then he made his famous report: "We have met the enemy, and they are ours."

The town of Erie is best known for building the ships used in this battle. But there's a lot to do in Erie. Many people enjoy its sandy lakeshore. They play in the sand and waves. Or they just gaze out across Lake Erie.

A brig is a sailing ship with 2 masts and square sails.

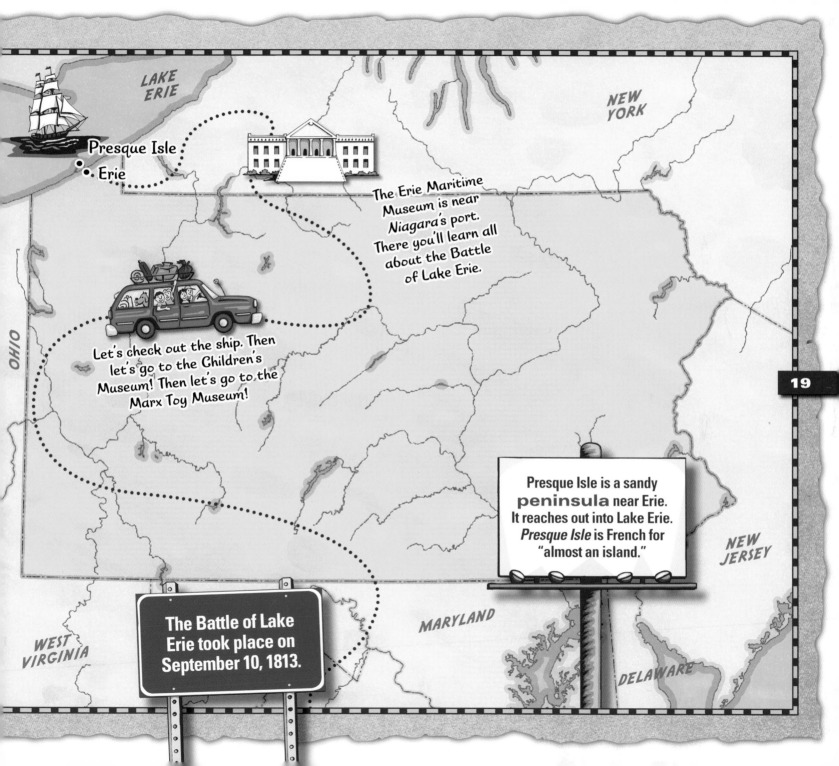

LAKE ERIE

NEW YORK

Presque Isle

Erie

The Erie Maritime Museum is near Niagara's port. There you'll learn all about the Battle of Lake Erie.

OHIO

Let's check out the ship. Then let's go to the Children's Museum! Then let's go to the Marx Toy Museum!

Presque Isle is a sandy **peninsula** near Erie. It reaches out into Lake Erie. *Presque Isle* is French for "almost an island."

NEW JERSEY

WEST VIRGINIA

The Battle of Lake Erie took place on September 10, 1813.

MARYLAND

DELAWARE

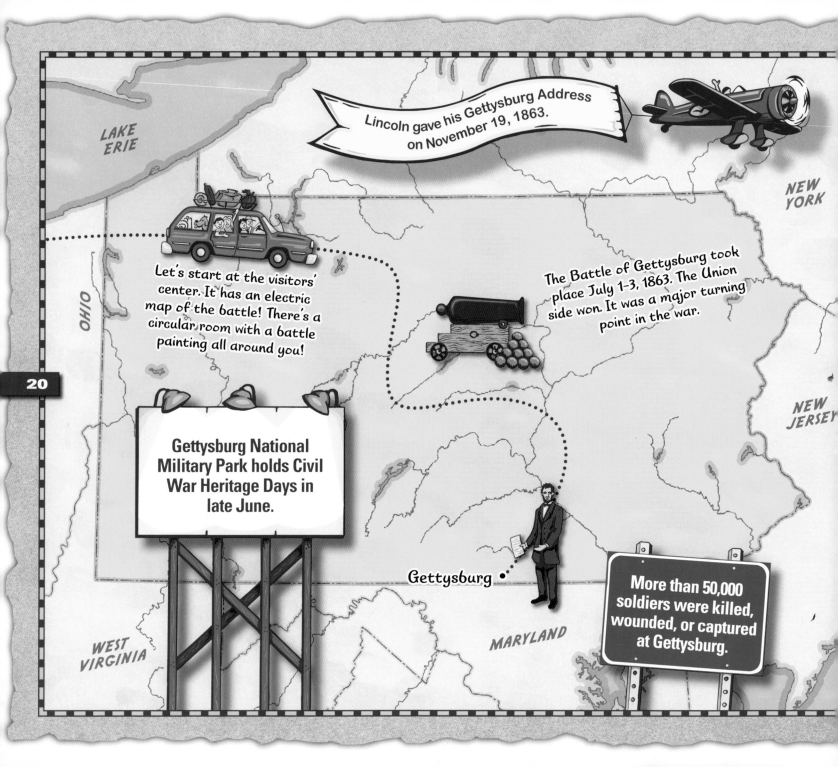

Lincoln gave his Gettysburg Address on November 19, 1863.

Let's start at the visitors' center. It has an electric map of the battle! There's a circular room with a battle painting all around you!

The Battle of Gettysburg took place July 1-3, 1863. The Union side won. It was a major turning point in the war.

Gettysburg National Military Park holds Civil War Heritage Days in late June.

Gettysburg

More than 50,000 soldiers were killed, wounded, or captured at Gettysburg.

LAKE ERIE

NEW YORK

OHIO

NEW JERSEY

WEST VIRGINIA

MARYLAND

Gettysburg and the Civil War

Look out over the rolling fields of Gettysburg. Thousands of soldiers died here. They were fighting the Civil War (1861–1865). Northern and Southern states fought this war over slavery.

Pennsylvania and other Northern states opposed slavery. Southern states wanted to keep slavery. This led to war. The North formed the Union side. Southern states pulled away and formed the Confederacy.

A bloody, three-day battle took place at Gettysburg. Part of the battlefield was made into a cemetery. President Abraham Lincoln spoke there. His famous speech is called the Gettysburg Address.

Scenic Gettysburg seems so peaceful. It's hard to imagine there was a battle here.

This mine is a fun place to visit. But you might not like to work here!

Anthracite (hard) coal is mined in eastern Pennsylvania. Bituminous (soft) coal is mined in western Pennsylvania.

Tour-Ed Mine in Tarentum

First, put on your hard hat. Then go deep into the coal mine. A real miner shows you how miners once worked. You're visiting the Tour-Ed Mine in Tarentum!

Pennsylvania's coal **industry** grew after the Civil War. Miners dug tons of coal from the ground. Railroads carried the coal to major cities.

Factories began using coal as a fuel. This helped the iron and steel industries grow. Pittsburgh soon became the country's top steel maker. Other factories made leather, cloth, glass, and cement.

The state is still a top coal producer. Pennsylvania also mines iron, oil, and natural gas.

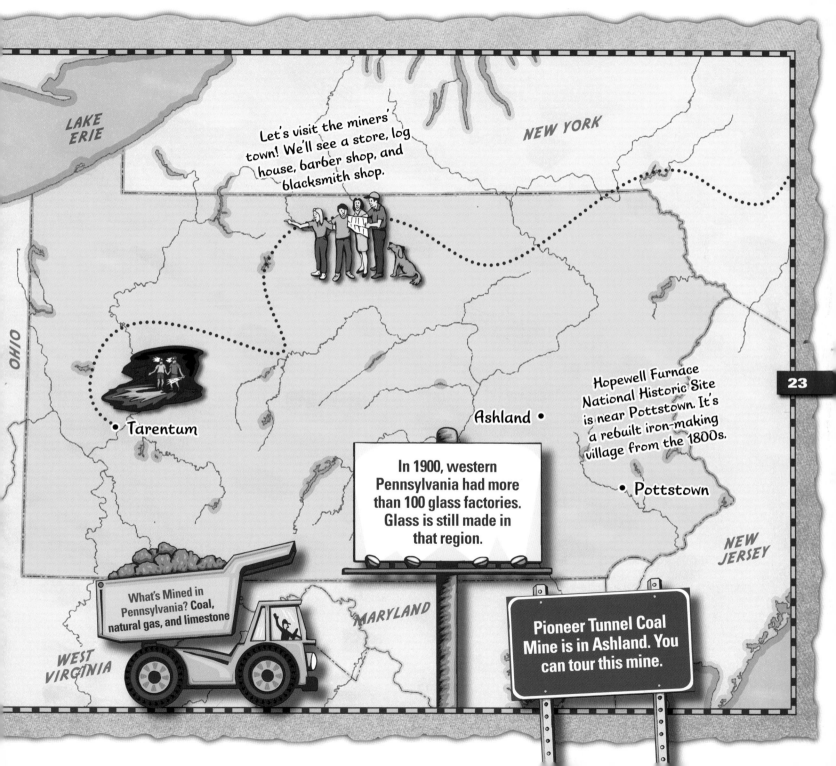

LAKE ERIE

NEW YORK

Let's visit the miners' town! We'll see a store, log house, barber shop, and blacksmith shop.

OHIO

Tarentum

Ashland •

Hopewell Furnace National Historic Site is near Pottstown. It's a rebuilt iron-making village from the 1800s.

In 1900, western Pennsylvania had more than 100 glass factories. Glass is still made in that region.

• Pottstown

NEW JERSEY

What's Mined in Pennsylvania? Coal, natural gas, and limestone

MARYLAND

WEST VIRGINIA

Pioneer Tunnel Coal Mine is in Ashland. You can tour this mine.

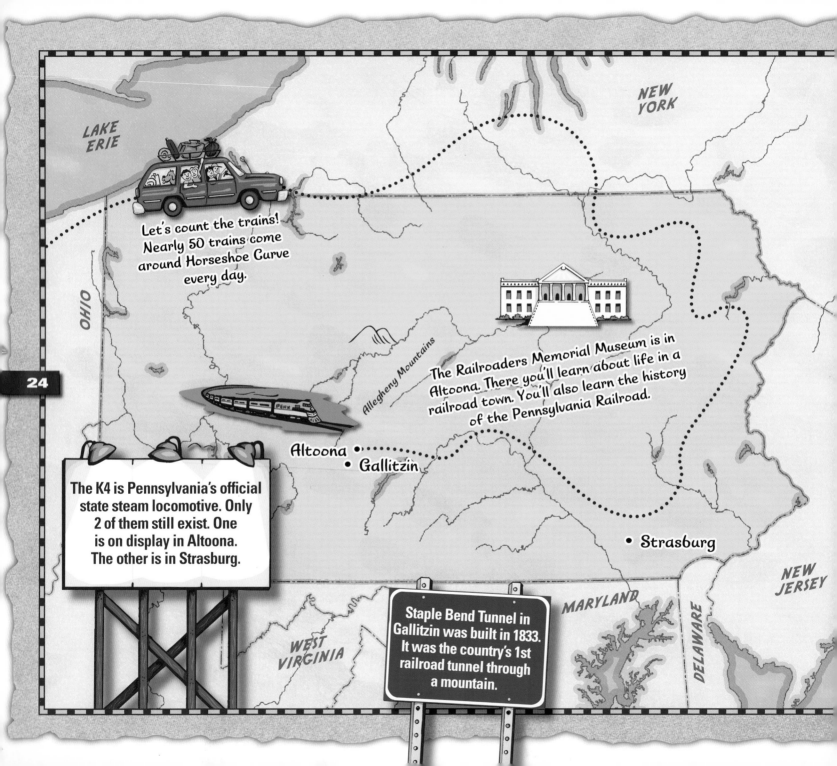

Let's count the trains! Nearly 50 trains come around Horseshoe Curve every day.

The Railroaders Memorial Museum is in Altoona. There you'll learn about life in a railroad town. You'll also learn the history of the Pennsylvania Railroad.

The K4 is Pennsylvania's official state steam locomotive. Only 2 of them still exist. One is on display in Altoona. The other is in Strasburg.

Staple Bend Tunnel in Gallitzin was built in 1833. It was the country's 1st railroad tunnel through a mountain.

NEW YORK

LAKE ERIE

OHIO

Allegheny Mountains

Altoona

Gallitzin

Strasburg

NEW JERSEY

MARYLAND

DELAWARE

WEST VIRGINIA

Trains at Altoona's Horseshoe Curve

Toot, toot! Clank, clank! Around the curve they come. The trains are screeching around Horseshoe Curve. Just hop on the hillside train car. Then ride up the hill. You'll have a great view of the curving tracks.

It was hard to build train tracks here. The Allegheny Mountains are really steep. Workers built the tracks in big loopy curves. That way, trains could climb the steep slopes.

Horseshoe Curve opened for train travel in 1854. At last, trains could get over the mountains. Then people could ship goods across the state.

All aboard! An early train travels around Horseshoe Curve.

Altoona was a major center for the Pennsylvania Railroad. Train cars were built and repaired there. More than 15,000 residents once worked for the railroad.

Check out the Carnegie Science Center! These young visitors are touring the SciQuest room.

The Discovery Center of Science and Technology is in Bethlehem.

Pittsburgh's Carnegie Science Center

Design and launch a rocket. Create some video cartoons. See hissing cockroaches and learn how weather works. You're exploring the Carnegie Science Center!

This museum is named after Andrew Carnegie. He formed his Carnegie Steel Company in 1899. Many of its mills were in the Pittsburgh area. Pittsburgh became a major steelmaking center. Many famous buildings were made with Pittsburgh steel. Carnegie sold his steel company in 1901. It grew into today's U.S. Steel Corporation. Carnegie made millions of dollars. He gave much of that money to charity. It was used for building museums and libraries.

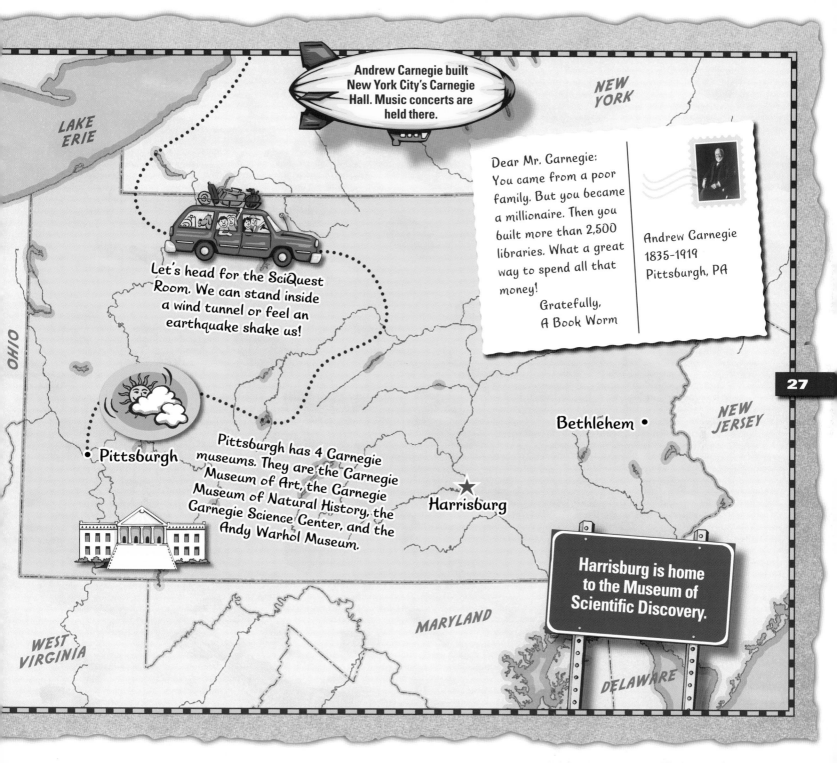

Andrew Carnegie built New York City's Carnegie Hall. Music concerts are held there.

NEW YORK

LAKE ERIE

Dear Mr. Carnegie:
You came from a poor family. But you became a millionaire. Then you built more than 2,500 libraries. What a great way to spend all that money!

Gratefully,
A Book Worm

Andrew Carnegie
1835-1919
Pittsburgh, PA

Let's head for the SciQuest Room. We can stand inside a wind tunnel or feel an earthquake shake us!

OHIO

NEW JERSEY

Bethlehem •

Pittsburgh

Pittsburgh has 4 Carnegie museums. They are the Carnegie Museum of Art, the Carnegie Museum of Natural History, the Carnegie Science Center, and the Andy Warhol Museum.

★ Harrisburg

Harrisburg is home to the Museum of Scientific Discovery.

WEST VIRGINIA

MARYLAND

DELAWARE

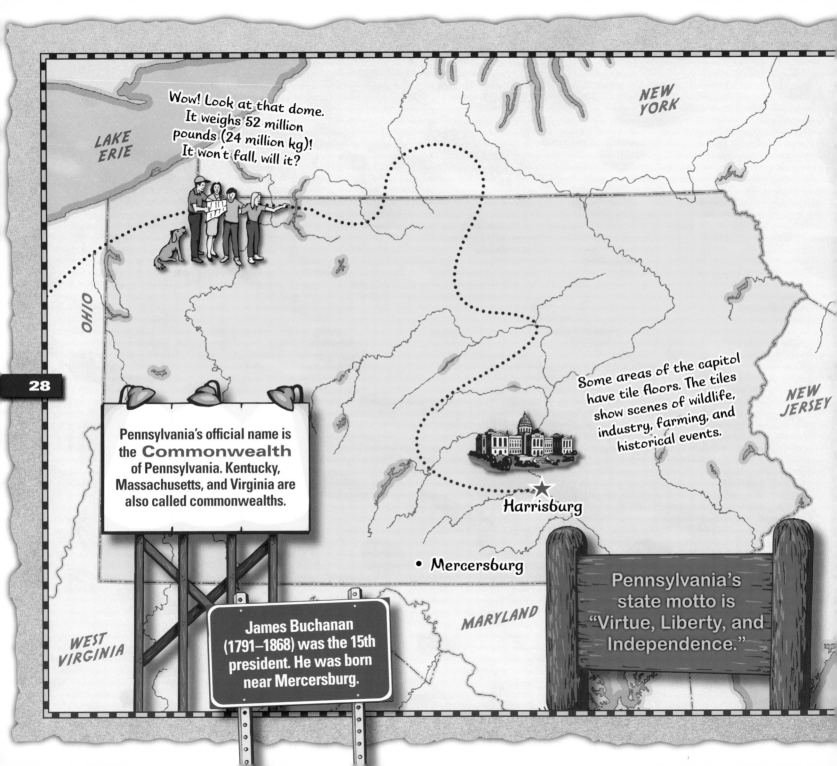

Wow! Look at that dome. It weighs 52 million pounds (24 million kg)! It won't fall, will it?

Some areas of the capitol have tile floors. The tiles show scenes of wildlife, industry, farming, and historical events.

Pennsylvania's official name is the **Commonwealth** of Pennsylvania. Kentucky, Massachusetts, and Virginia are also called commonwealths.

James Buchanan (1791–1868) was the 15th president. He was born near Mercersburg.

Pennsylvania's state motto is "Virtue, Liberty, and Independence."

LAKE ERIE

NEW YORK

OHIO

NEW JERSEY

★ Harrisburg

• Mercersburg

WEST VIRGINIA

MARYLAND

The State Capitol in Harrisburg

You'll love visiting the state capitol. It looks like a grand palace! Just walk into the big, round central area. Look up, and you'll see almost 4,000 lights. Above you rises the huge, curved dome.

This is the main state government building. Pennsylvania has three branches of government. One branch makes the laws. Its members meet in the capitol. Another branch carries out the laws. It's headed by the governor. Judges make up the third branch. They study the laws. Then they decide whether someone has broken a law.

How would you like to work here? Pennsylvania lawmakers meet in the capitol.

Welcome to Harrisburg, the capital of Pennsylvania!

Look at all those tomatoes! Tomatoes are an important crop in Pennsylvania.

Perrydell Farm Dairy is in York. You can watch the cows being milked. Then you can see the milk poured into bottles.

The Pittston Tomato Festival

Watch out! Here comes a big one! Splat! Yuk!

You tried to duck out of the way. But you didn't duck fast enough. You've joined the big tomato fight! It's an event at the Pittston Tomato Festival.

Pittston is proud of its tomatoes. Lots of farmers in the area grow them. Mushrooms are the state's top crop, though. Pennsylvania grows more mushrooms than any other state. Corn and hay are important, too. Most of the corn becomes cattle feed.

Dairy cattle graze across eastern Pennsylvania. They produce tons of milk. Chickens and eggs are valuable farm products, too.

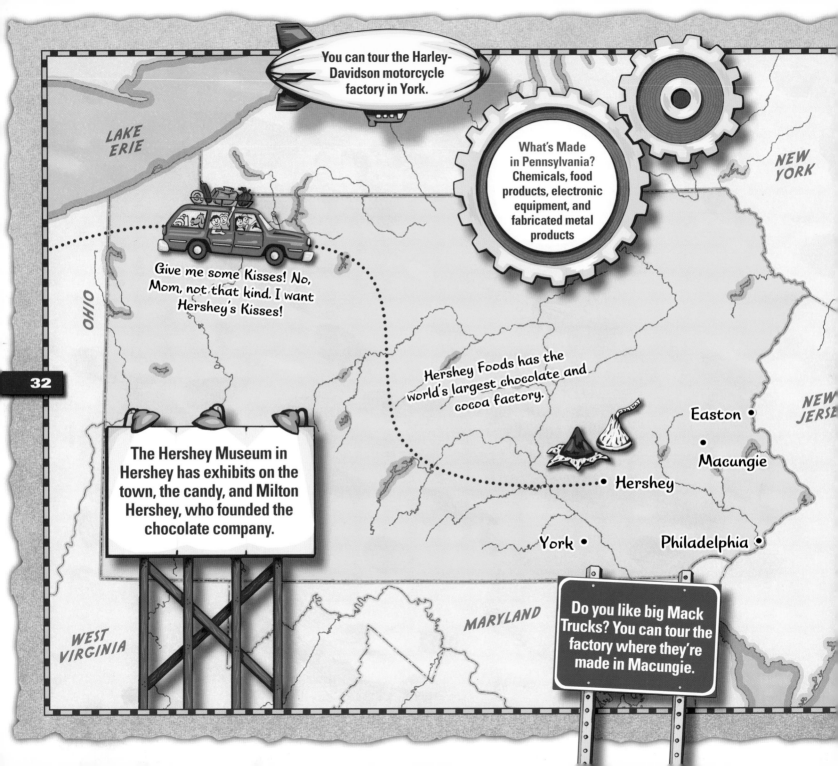

Hershey's Chocolate World

Do you like chocolate? Then you'll love Hershey's Chocolate World. Guess what city it's in. Hershey! You can take a chocolate-making tour there.

First you'll walk through a jungle. Cocoa beans are growing there. Then you'll see the chocolate factory. That's where the cocoa beans are made into chocolate. Finally, you'll get to eat some delicious samples. Yum!

Foods are important factory goods in Pennsylvania. Food plants make chocolate, bread, cookies, and pretzels. Some factories package mushrooms and meats. Chemicals are the state's leading factory products. They include medicine and paint. Pennsylvania makes Crayola crayons, too!

Yum, I can smell the chocolate from here. I'll race you to the samples!

Visit the Crayola crayon factory in Easton. It makes more than 2 billion crayons every year!

WHACK! And that ball's out of here! These guys celebrate a home run at the 2004 Little League World Series.

Do you like amusement parks with thrilling rides? Pennsylvania has more than 15 parks like this!

The Little League World Series

Kids are here from Mexico, Europe, and Asia. They're all ready to play baseball. It's the Little League World Series!

Little League baseball began in Williamsport in 1939. In time, it spread all over the world. Now Williamsport holds the Little League World Series. Some of the world's best players take part.

Pennsylvanians enjoy big-league sports, too. But many people have fun in other ways. They go swimming or hiking. They climb mountains or trek through forests. Some like visiting historic sites and museums. There's something for everyone in Pennsylvania!

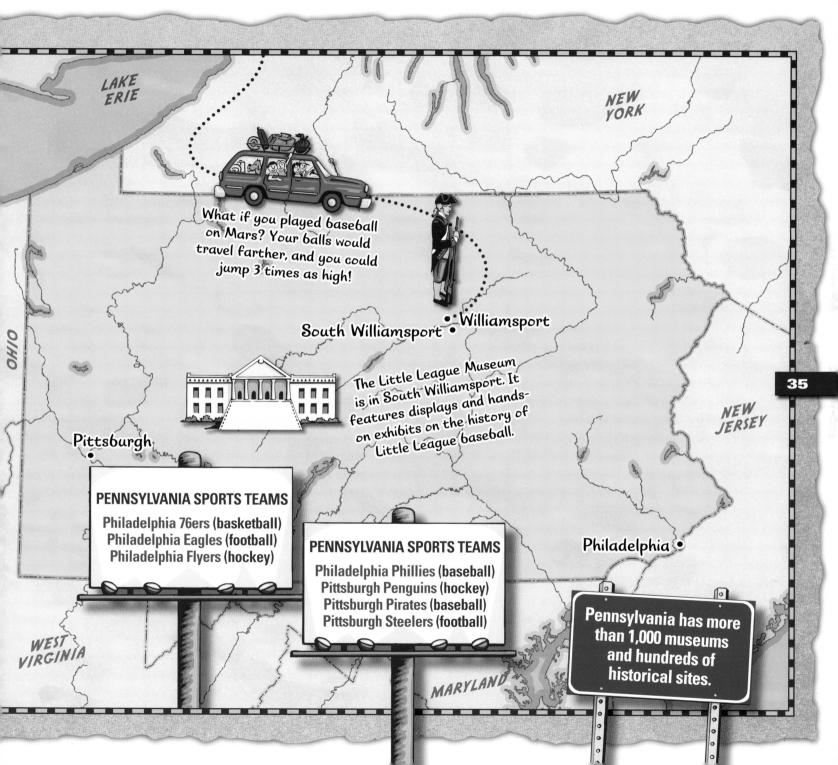

LAKE ERIE

NEW YORK

OHIO

What if you played baseball on Mars? Your balls would travel farther, and you could jump 3 times as high!

South Williamsport • • Williamsport

The Little League Museum is in South Williamsport. It features displays and hands-on exhibits on the history of Little League baseball.

Pittsburgh •

NEW JERSEY

PENNSYLVANIA SPORTS TEAMS

Philadelphia 76ers (basketball)
Philadelphia Eagles (football)
Philadelphia Flyers (hockey)

PENNSYLVANIA SPORTS TEAMS

Philadelphia Phillies (baseball)
Pittsburgh Penguins (hockey)
Pittsburgh Pirates (baseball)
Pittsburgh Steelers (football)

Philadelphia •

Pennsylvania has more than 1,000 museums and hundreds of historical sites.

WEST VIRGINIA

MARYLAND

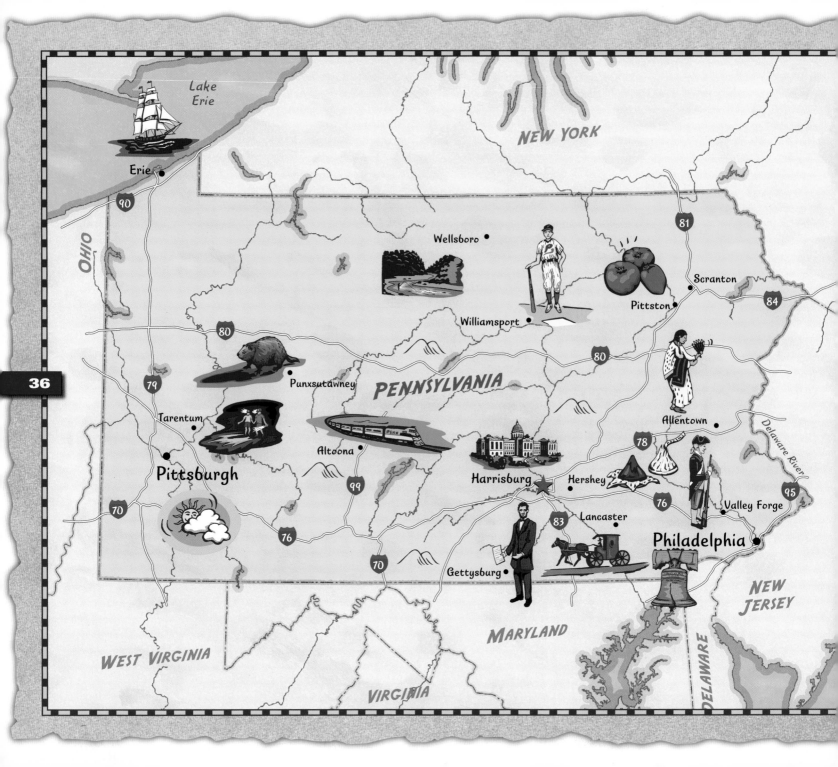

Lake Erie

Erie

NEW YORK

OHIO

Wellsboro

Scranton

Pittston

Williamsport

PENNSYLVANIA

Punxsutawney

Allentown

Tarentum

Altoona

Harrisburg

Hershey

Pittsburgh

Valley Forge

Lancaster

Philadelphia

Gettysburg

Delaware River

NEW JERSEY

MARYLAND

DELAWARE

WEST VIRGINIA

VIRGINIA

90
81
84
80
79
80
78
99
95
70
76
76
83
70

OUR TRIP

We visited many amazing places on our trip! We also met a lot of interesting people along the way. Look at the map on the left. Use your finger to trace all the places we have been.

What is called the Grand Canyon of Pennsylvania? See page 7 for the answer.

How long have people been watching Punxsutawney Phil? Page 8 has the answer.

When did Pennsylvania enter the Union? See page 15 for the answer.

When did the Liberty Bell crack? Look on page 16 for the answer.

Where is the Museum of Scientific Discovery located? Page 27 has the answer.

What is Pennsylvania's state motto? Turn to page 28 for the answer.

What Pennsylvania town holds a mushroom festival? Look on page 31 for the answer.

How many Crayola crayons are produced each year? Turn to page 33 for the answer.

That was a great trip! We have traveled all over Pennsylvania. There are a few places we didn't have time for, though. Next time, we plan to visit the Houdini Museum in Scranton. Visitors learn all about famous magician and escape artist Harry Houdini. The museum features items related to Houdini's life and career. Some date back to the late 1800s!

More Places to Visit in Pennsylvania

WORDS TO KNOW

canyons (KAN-yuhnz) deep valleys worn through by rivers

colonists (KOL-uh-nists) people who settle a new land for their home country

colony (KOL-uh-nee) a land with ties to a parent country

commonwealth (KOM-uhn-welth) a state or nation founded for the people's common good

immigrants (IM-uh-gruhnts) people who leave their home country and move to another country

industry (IN-duh-stree) a type of business

mercenaries (MUR-suh-ner-eez) soldiers who are paid to fight for a foreign army

peninsula (puh-NIN-suh-luh) a piece of land completely surrounded by water

plateau (pla-TOH) land that is high and somewhat level

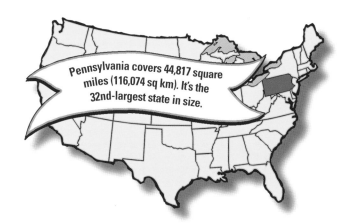

Pennsylvania covers 44,817 square miles (116,074 sq km). It's the 32nd-largest state in size.

STATE SYMBOLS

State animal: White-tailed deer

State beautification plant: Crown vetch

State beverage: Milk

State bird: Ruffed grouse

State dog: Great Dane

State electric locomotive: GCI 4859 electric locomotive

State fish: Brook trout

State flower: Mountain laurel

State fossil: *Phacops rana*

State insect: Firefly

State ship: U.S. brig *Niagara*

State steam locomotive: K4 steam locomotive

State tree: Hemlock

State flag

State seal

STATE SONG

"Pennsylvania"

Words and music by Eddie Khoury and Ronnie Bonner

Pennsylvania, Pennsylvania,
Mighty is your name,
Steeped in glory and tradition,
Object of acclaim.
Where brave men fought the foe of freedom,
Tyranny decried,
'Til the bell of independence
Filled the countryside.

Chorus:
Pennsylvania, Pennsylvania,
May your future be
filled with honor everlasting
as your history.

Pennsylvania, Pennsylvania,
Blessed by God's own hand,
Birthplace of a mighty nation,
Keystone of the land.
Where first our country's flag unfolded,
Freedom to proclaim,
May the voices of tomorrow
glorify your name.

(Chorus)

FAMOUS PEOPLE

Anderson, Marian (1897–1993), concert singer

Brown, Marc (1946–), children's author and illustrator

Buchanan, James (1791–1868), 15th U.S. president

Carson, Rachel (1907–1964), author and environmentalist

Cassatt, Mary (1844–1926), painter

Catalanotto, Peter (1959–), children's author and illustrator

Cosby, Bill (1937–), comedian and actor

Franklin, Benjamin (1706–1790), inventor, author, and patriot during the American Revolution

Graham, Martha (1894–1991), dancer and choreographer

Hershey, Milton S. (1857–1945), founder of the Hershey Chocolate Company

Jackson, Reggie (1946–), baseball player

Kelly, Gene (1912–1996), dancer and actor

Konigsburg, E. L. (1930–), children's author

Mead, Margaret (1901–1978), anthropologist

Montana, Joe (1956–), football player

Mott, Lucretia (1793–1880), leader of the abolitionist and women's rights movements

Penn, William (1644–1718), founder of Pennsylvania

Rogers, Fred (1928–2003), "Mr. Rogers"

Ross, Betsy (1752–1836), patriot during the American Revolution

Stewart, James (1908–1997), actor

Wyeth, Andrew (1917–), painter

TO FIND OUT MORE

At the Library

Franchino, Vicky. *Betsy Ross: Patriot.* Chanhassen, Minn.: The Child's World, 2003.

Kane, Kristen, and Laura Knorr (illustrator). *K Is for Keystone: A Pennsylvania Alphabet.* Chelsea, Mich.: Sleeping Bear Press, 2003.

Ryan, Pam Muñoz, and Brian Selznick (illustrator). *When Marian Sang: The True Recital of Marian Anderson: The Voice of a Century.* New York: Scholastic Press, 2002.

Schanzer, Rosalyn. *How Ben Franklin Stole the Lightning.* New York: HarperCollins, 2003.

Wilson, Jon. *The Liberty Bell: The Sounds of Freedom.* Chanhassen, Minn.: The Child's World, 1999.

On the Web

Visit our home page for lots of links about Pennsylvania:
http://www.childsworld.com/links

Note to Parents, Teachers, and Librarians: We routinely verify our Web links to make sure they are safe, active sites—so encourage your readers to check them out!

Places to Visit or Contact

The Historical Society of Pennsylvania
1300 Locust Street
Philadelphia, PA 19107
215/732-2600
For more information about the history of Pennsylvania

Pennsylvania Department of Community and Economic Development
4th Floor, Commonwealth Keystone Building
400 North Street
Harrisburg, PA 17120-0225
800/237-4363
For more information about traveling in Pennsylvania

INDEX

Bye, Keystone State.
We had a great time.
We'll come back soon!